ISBN: 978-0-578-54154-9

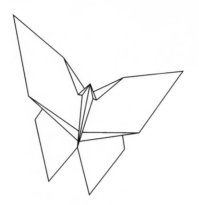

A GUIDE

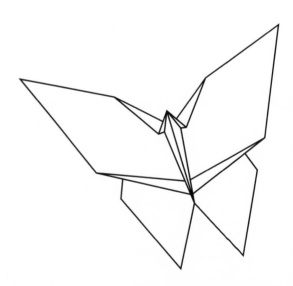

TABLE OF CONTENTS

INTRODUCTION

Gary Brantley II

I have always wanted to write a book on my experiences, but only after I was retired and on a beach somewhere looking at a beautiful sunset and clear blue water. I imagined myself far removed from the workforce, reflecting on a long career. Over the last few years, I realized that it might be better to capture my experience now while it is fresh and I am in the midst of it.

I was thrust into a leadership role at a very young age—some would say even before I was ready. I have worked for small organizations and large organizations. One thing I can say is there are no shortcuts to becoming a great leader. Every experience that I have encountered played a pivotal role in the full development of my leadership style.

I have transformed myself several times over the course of my career, and I am still growing. Transformation is a never-ending process if you aspire to be a change agent. In fact, every leader must be a change agent because you need that skill set to revamp an organization.

As a leader in technology for more than twenty years, I have always found it interesting that I ended up in organizations that were struggling with the process of transformation. Usually the first thing leaders want to do when they get hired is put their imprint on the organization or department they were hired to le

I have always wondered why leaders are in such a rush to transform an organization without being a part of the entity long enough to understand the true internal needs. This simple but important question has resonated with me my entire career. It resonated with me so much that I sought out leaders across the country to provide insight on the difficulty of organizational transformation.

Transformation itself requires a complete metamorphosis. Imagine how hard it is for you to transform yourself—let alone an entire organization. You can go to the gym for years and not see the type of change you are looking for in your body. I remember embarking on a journey to change my body so it resembled a superhero's. I watched countless workout videos and infomercials on how to accomplish this goal. It seemed fairly simple. In six weeks I would become a professional bodybuilder, having shed every ounce of useless fat on my body. In my mind, all I needed to do was watch the videos and follow the routine.

Six weeks passed, and needless to say, I did not look anything like what the videos had advertised to me. This was supposed to be a simple transformation with a strict, easy-to-follow regimen. This is often how we act as leaders when we enter organizations for the first time. We come in and approach it as if transformation can take place quickly. We make promises without stepping one foot inside the organization or understanding its culture. After speaking with several CEOs and C-suite leaders, I have come to the conclusion that even the most experienced leaders struggle with organizational transformation simply because it impacts people personally.

Before you can transform any organization, you truly need to master the art of personally transforming yourself. Focusing on self-improvement and having a complete understanding of yourself and your purpose is discomforting. When leaders understand the discomfort that goes along with transforming organizations, it becomes an invaluable guide. Transformation comes with a lot of uncertainty, rejection, and sometimes plenty of embarrassment. I am a big Animal Planet fan. Ever since I was a little boy, I have always been fascinated with the wildlife found on earth. Different animal species' habits and practices can teach us great things, but animals that go through a metamorphic process teach us valuable lessons about transformation.

The caterpillar is probably the most popular example of an animal that goes through a metamorphosis. However, when you look at other species that go through complete metamorphoses, you find commonalities that are consistent among several different species. The one thing that is clear is that every species follows a consistent process. During every transformation, each species must eat. Just a little while ago, I talked about my workout experiences and the transformation that I was expecting. One very important step I left out in my example is the nutritional component.

My parents worked extremely hard for what they acquired in life. They taught me to be respectful and to work hard. I was able to see in my parents that if I worked hard, put time in, and followed a consistent regimen, then I could transform myself into anything I put my mind to. Hard work was the foundation on which I was raised. I watched my dad and both my grandfathers work tirelessly to provide for their families. I saw this as a blueprint for success. I watched hard work lead to positive and productive transformations.

I have never been a big city guy. I grew up in a small town in Northeast Ohio. Youngstown was known for its steel production. No place in the United States of America could produce steel like this little town that bordered the state of Pennsylvania, that used iron and carbon to produce some of the world's finest steel. After the steel was formed, it was molded into various shapes and forms. The manufacturers shipped the steel all over the world and used it to create many of the new inventions of the time. Companies used steel to create large athletic stadiums and structures that still stand today. Our town was full of pride and was masterful at producing steel. The transformation process had to be followed without deviation, and my hometown executed this art with consistency. I tell this story to highlight the importance process and culture when implementing long lasting transformational change.

At some point in life, everyone and everything will go through a transformation process. This is especially true in corporations, government entities, and educational institutions. I have had the opportunity to work and experience both successful and unsuccessful transformations in each of these industries. At the conclusion of most transformational initiatives, the reasons for success or failure are very apparent.

The 7-step process we will explore in this book is rooted in personal experience combined with research and years of C-level expertise. The 7-step process is designed to be used as a guide during the course of organizational transformation. Transformation is a never-ending process in organizations and in some instances the lack of successful transformation has left them unable to operate.

My goal is that each chapter, you will uncover a clearer understanding of the organizational transformation process. Transformation is a process that naturally resides within us. Transformation in an organizational setting can either be natural and organic or artificial and forced. However, it must be intentional. These guiding principles will arm you with the tools to effectively engage in a natural and authentic organizational transformation process in both your professional and personal life.

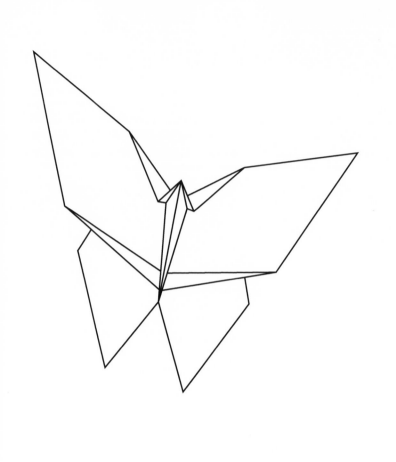
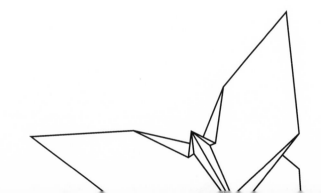

CHAPTER 1

CULTURE

Organizational culture is not created by one individual.

I remember years ago when I first heard the word culture. I was working at IBM as a network administrator, providing desktop support for the Goodyear Tire & Rubber Company in Akron, Ohio. I was just 19 years old at the time with a head full of hair and the energy of a bronco. This was my first real job, and I was soaking up every opportunity to learn as much as I could. I was a young African American boy looking to enter a field where no one looked like me. As a young man who was just entering into the corporate arena, I paid attention to every little detail. I was fascinated to see what I perceived to be so many successful people in one building.

From the time I entered the building, I noticed that everyone was impeccably dressed. I did not realize at the time that this was a reflection of the culture of the company. I had never even heard the word culture in the corporate world. In my mind the word culture was reflective of race norms. To me the word focused on ideas, behaviors, beliefs, and traditions that were shared by different ethnic races. I had no idea what culture meant when business leaders used it to describe or refer to organizations. However, I would soon find out.

Every day that I walked into the building, something new would catch my attention. The organization provided meals in house for its employees, and the employees were extremely sociable. This setup encouraged the employees to engage with each other in conversation. Obviously, the employees discussed work, but they would also communicate with each other on a deeper and more personal level. As I continued to observe, I also noticed the company supplied its facilities with workout equipment, which was unheard of in my experience.

I was so taken aback by these amenities that one day I asked the manager of my department why the company provided meals and workout equipment for employees. He simply replied, "This is part of the culture that we work hard to create here." Again, this particular company forged a tight-knit group of employees that not only worked together but also had deeper personal relationships beyond the workplace.

As the years went by, I continued to hear the word

culture used in a variety of ways and in different situations. It wasn't until I had the opportunity to join a project team that was taking the entire organization to a new network architecture that I heard the word culture used as a part of a strategy to effect organizational change.

The management team was very focused on the culture of the organization during the planning phase of the project. They wanted to make sure that the project team was aware of what that meant, but I was very green and didn't understand. I couldn't comprehend why we weren't devoting more attention to the technical side. I remember going home that evening wondering, "Why are they so worried about the culture of this organization on a network conversion project?" Needless to say, I would find out shortly why we were so focused on culture. The culture of the organization became the blueprint for how we would roll out the new architecture. The project became less about the technical aspect, and more about how we would transition the employees (our customers) into a completely new system. You see, this was an organization that was accustomed to operating a certain way for more than 20 years. The employees were seasoned and, on average, had been with the organization for 15 years or more. However, unbeknownst to me, many of the employees had voiced their displeasure about moving to a new system, as they were skeptical about the success of the conversion.

As the planning efforts continued, we were focused on providing the best customer service possible for all of the employees who would be affected. I began to really understand just how sensitive a project this was going to be. I suddenly realized that the project we were working on would be a huge culture shift for the organization. I knew that the manner in which the project team handled the culture shift would be the key to its successful implementation.

I spent years furthering my education. We coded, designed, engineered, and even collaborated throughout my educational experience, but we never covered the ability to navigate organizational culture in the midst of transformation. Organizational culture is comprised of values, and as I learned, these values and beliefs have a strong influence on the employees in the organization. The values and beliefs of the organization guide how people behave, act, dress, and perform daily on the job. I was never taught any of this as a computer science major in college. These are valuable lessons that can only be learned on the job. The organization had developed its own belief system that the project team had to take into account in order to influence change. I watched as we took very detailed steps to ensure that we were very careful in our communication during this conversion.

The management team had a solid plan. They focused on the following questions:

- Who are the employees that have the most peer-to-peer influence on other employees in the organization?

- How can we show these employees that the future is better than the present?

- How can we implement a reward and recognition system that is aligned with change?

- How can we strengthen communication before and after the change?

- How can we manage the emotional sensitivity to change by controlling the narrative?

- How can we manage fear?

As you can see, the focus was less about the technical aspects of the project and more about managing the current culture. Don't get me wrong; we spent a lot of time preparing technically for the project because that, too, can cause major problems and impact emotional stability. We were equally balanced in our focus, and that was an instrumental component in the success of the project.

Organizational culture is not created by one individual. We make a big mistake when we credit one particular employee with forming the culture for an entire department or organization. Culture in an organization is formed by a series of factors. These include demands placed on the organization, outcomes and expectations, leadership values, and organizational assumptions. **Assumptions** play a large role in the type of culture that exists within an organization. In organizational culture assumptions are invisible, accepted beliefs. They have the potential to be very dangerous if they are not interpreted correctly and handled carefully. Let's go back to the example of how we prepared the Goodyear Tire & Rubber Company for the transformational change it was about to go through. Many employees had assumptions on how this change would take place and whether the outcome would be successful based on the strategy they assumed was in place.

The interesting thing about assumptions is that they are rarely questioned once they are accepted. When transforming organizations, you must understand what your organization is assuming and whether the assumptions are shared. In most cases they are not just an individual's but shared by many. When you take on the work of organizational transformation, make sure you have a solid understanding of the basis for forming assumptions. Once you learn how they are formed in the organization, you can implement strategies to use those assumptions to carry out the transformation process.

My first real job introduced to me the word *culture*. As I continued to progress through my career, I noticed the word *culture* constantly being used when discussing any organizational transformation taking place. I have worked for both public and private companies in my career. Oftentimes people like to say there is a difference between the two sectors. While I have found that to be true in some cases, the one constant I have found is that understanding the culture is critical because culture doesn't care which sector you are in.

I remember my first public sector job earlier in my career. I was excited to work for the government. I was beaming with pride, and my heart was full of joy. I was giving back to the city and state that had invested in me. I had the opportunity to really help the community, and I knew the work was going to be rewarding. I was in my first Chief Information Officer role, and I was approaching everything with a ton of energy. This was also my first major leadership role. I was privileged to step into leadership at a very young age, and this would be my first true test of leading others.

I walked into my first meeting with all of the C-level executives prepared to highlight the many initiatives I had planned for the next few years. During the meeting, several of my peers were discussing how they planned to approach the year. They were all veterans of the organization, and I was the youngest person in the room by about 20 years. It is important to know that this was a public organization with multiple unions and bargaining-unit employees. As we all know, unions can be extremely difficult to work with. Even the most seasoned leaders can fail when dealing with a unionized workforce. Union leaders and their representatives have mastered the art of negotiating. Nothing in college could have prepared me for what I was about to take on. Many people say experience is the greatest teacher, and I didn't have much of it.

As the meeting continued, the agenda was approaching my plans for Information Technology and how we would execute those initiatives. I began to present my plan for a complete overhaul of the current technology. I was about three minutes into the presentation, and I saw nothing but blank stares across the room. I could sense that the team was not receiving my plan very well.

I paused my presentation, and to check the climate in the room, I asked if anyone had any questions up to that point. The president of one of the unions sternly said, "I will make sure we send equipment back to your office addressed specifically to you." As you can imagine, the look on my face was one of pure shock and embarrassment. This was my first real teachable moment in leadership and transformation. I still reflect on that moment to this day, and find myself constantly overanalyzing my thought process at that time. Some would say that I should have known better, but it's clear to me that you cannot skip any steps to becoming a great leader. Exceptional leadership has no shortcuts, and no matter how big or small, every lesson learned is valuable and can be used for improvement.

Let's examine what went wrong with my presentation and what strategies I could have employed to avoid the disaster that took place:

- Take time to really learn and study the organization

being transformed. I did not understand the culture enough to immediately make or even discuss the progressive transformation I wanted to implement. Find out who your blockers and your potential champions are. The more information you have, the more you can successfully strategize for the transformation.

- Take time to listen effectively while simultaneously exercising patience. I rushed through and did not take the time to talk to employees and key stakeholders of the organization. It seems simple, but I see this mistake made all the time. Use time to your advantage because it really can be your friend. The more conversations you have, the easier your path will be to transformation.

- Eliminate the art of surprise. Most, if not all, of the people in the room should have some idea of what you plan to present because of the conversations that have previously taken place. Everyone in the room should feel like an active participant in the

- transformational plan.

- Find a seasoned champion on the executive team. I needed at least one person at the table who strongly supported the plan that I was presenting. The team needed to see someone they trusted and respected support the plan. Even at the C-suite level, there are leaders and followers. In my experiences I have learned that there are leaders among leaders. You must have a plan of action to gain their support.

- Have a complete understanding of organizational politics (which I'll discuss more in later chapters). Every organization has politics you must navigate through. Navigating politics is a part of being in any leadership position, but it is most critical when taking on the task of leading organizational transformation.

Had I just employed those five basic strategies, my presentation would have, at a minimum, created positive dialogue, which would have led to a successful presentation. Understanding culture was critical to the success of my presentation, and I lacked a complete understanding of their basic workplace culture. In leadership you must constantly study the behavior of the people who are a part of the organization. When you walk into an organization as I did, you must have the ability to adjust to the culture. Flexibility and the ability to adapt to organizational culture can be the difference between keeping yourself employed and finding yourself without a job.

When I walk into organizations now, I start to immediately identify cultural norms and behaviors. This information becomes a key part of my strategy for transforming and leading organizations. Employees in organizations have beliefs, working systems they abide by, and ingrained habits that must first be understood. Moving too quickly to make change will be counterproductive and harmful to your ability to transform an organization. In the later chapters, we will discuss longevity and time, and show how critical they are to the success of organizational transformation.

Oftentimes, companies feel there isn't a need for transformation. You must understand the amount of transformation necessary for the organization you join. The organizational transformation should be aligned to the needs of the business. However, you must first understand the business and its culture. As a leader, have you ever taken the time to really look into what your company values about its employees? When you take the time to examine what that is, you will begin to see that it has a lot to do with how the culture is formed. As we move on to discuss other steps that will guide you on your mission for successful organizational transformation, understand that it starts with having a deep understanding of the culture of the organization you are transforming. Take the opportunity to learn about your organization. As I stated in the introduction, many times we are in such a rush to make a difference and to put our imprint on the organization that we completely miss the mark. Do not make the mistake of making promises before making an entrance or making introductions. You cannot change what you do not completely understand. Understanding culture can be complex. Take the time to unravel it layer by layer, and watch how much critical information you obtain that will help you set your strategic plan.

CHAPTER 2

RELATIONSHIPS

Build strong relationships tied to your business strategy.

Most people say that establishing strong relationships in business organizations is an essential part of your success. A business relationship is defined as the way in which two or more employees or stakeholders connect. It is the state of being connected. As we move throughout this chapter, I will walk you through how to find and build relationships that guide you in transforming your organization. This chapter may be the most important in the guide to organizational transformation because nothing in business is successfully accomplished without strong relationships.

If you have lived in this world long enough, you understand that relationships are not created overnight. They take time, a great deal of patience, a deep understanding of one another, and in some cases, a little bit of luck. Building strong relationships leads to opportunities and personal growth inside and outside of your organization. To transform organizations, you need to build external and internal relationships. Often you will find external forces are key to driving your internal transformation. Whether I am out in the local community or in a completely different state, I am always looking to build strong relationships. This is important because you really never know when those relationships will pay dividends. As big as the world is, it can also be very small because of relationships. I have found some unexpected opportunities because of relationships I developed with no expectations. To put it another way, I had no idea how the relationships I built would benefit me immediately or down the road.

Building relationships should always remain a constant both in your personal and professional life. The art of relationship building should always be at the core of your business strategy. I often hear employees and organizational leaders who say, "I am not here to make friends or build any type of relationship. I am simply here to work and go home." This mind-set and approach is a mistake. You will not be successful in leading or transformation unless you are intentional about building relationships. You must think strategically about what relationships to build and cultivate. Some relationships will pay dividends immediately, but the majority of relationships will need to be leveraged later on in your transformational process. Prioritize the time you spend on building relationships, and make sure those relationships are aligned with the immediate goal you are trying to accomplish. This can be very difficult to navigate if you have not worked through understanding the culture of the organization, which was discussed in chapter 1. Once you understand the culture, you must next move on to building the relationships necessary to advance the agenda of transformation.

Business relationships in your organization must be reciprocal. The individual that you are building the relationship with must see value in it as well. Just like you want support from the relationships you build, the other party will want the same support in return. This is what I consider a silent expectation. Few people will ever shout at the top of their lungs that they expect you to support them, but if it is a genuine relationship, it will be necessary to do so at some point.

I know all too well how beneficial building strong relationships can be in leadership and in the midst of organizational transformation. A few years ago, I experienced firsthand how relationships are vital to the transformational process. Relationships need to be built across the organization. They can be established with coworkers, your employees, community stakeholders, and with your customers. It took me a while to realize how extensive the relationships needed to be in order to permeate throughout the organization.

I've watched leaders in the different organizations that I've had the privilege of being a part of use relationships to navigate change. I remember looking back, thinking none of what I was witnessing was taught to me in any college course. Only experience across several different organizations provided me with the blueprint for success. The amount of time that it takes to really build fruitful relationships and a supportive network can take years. I mentioned earlier that you must use time as your friend. It is very important as you enter into an organization that you temper expectations. I know leaders who desire to just walk into organizations with a ninety-day plan full of action items and changes they want to make. Most times the ninety-day plan is constructed after entering the organization. As a leader, if you have a plan (I suggest you have a plan) make sure that it involves a heavy dose of listening and a strategy that includes who you need to start building relationships with.

Remake Yourself and Be Transparent

Over time I have learned how to step out of my comfort zone to build relationships. It may come easy to some, but I personally know that is not always the case. I do not consider myself to be very outgoing and comfortable initiating conversations with new people. Therefore, I struggled with this aspect of my leadership development. I had to almost transform into a completely different person to effectuate relationship building. Like many others, I do not establish trust very easily. I was simply not interested in doing what it takes to build relationships. I had a lot of work ahead of me to improve in this area.

As I continued on throughout my leadership roles, I continued to struggle with relationship building. If you ask any person in my family about me, he or she will tell you, "Gary is not a man of many words unless he gets to know you." Even then my conversations with people were sparse. I considered myself to be a private person, and I did not want anyone I did not trust to know much about me. This was a very flawed way of thinking. **When you are a leader, you cannot completely close yourself off. You must be accessible and relatable.**

I remember hearing rumblings from my staff that I was not very friendly. I was shocked! I considered myself to be a very friendly person. I was actually somewhat offended by the assertion. As I took more time to consider their point of view, what I learned was very interesting and surprising. They did not feel it was because I was walking around screaming at my staff. Rather, people expected me to always speak to them— to take the time to really sit down with them and learn about their beliefs, interests, and goals. That realization was really a defining point in my transformation as a leader. Even when you think what you are doing is enough, you always need to strive to improve. I realized this was not just about me and my aspirations anymore. I was now in leadership, and I had to change things about myself quickly to thrive and more importantly, survive.

As a test case for myself, I started to really focus on my interactions with my staff and employees in different departments across the organization. I began to hone in on the following:

- Becoming intentional about my conversations with my staff and employees across the organization. Even when I did not feel like having conversations, I forced myself to have them.

- Focusing on how I presented myself. I needed to appear open and optimistic. My demeanor needed to change. I smiled even when the circumstances did not inspire me to smile.

- Strategized on how I could use the conversations and the relationships to my advantage. I used every conversation as an opportunity to see how my interactions affected my opportunities moving forward.

- Focused on the conversations around mutual interests that I shared with individuals I wanted to build relationships with.

Opening up is not easy. It only became easier for me when I became intentional about it. I am not saying that you need to be an open book, but it does help people relate to you a little better if you allow yourself to be somewhat vulnerable. I found that the more conversations I had with employees across the organization, the more I was able to hone in on the mutual interest we shared. The mutual interest was not always deep or complex. It could be as simple as sports or music. What I found was that you can open yourself up to build relationships without exposing areas of your life that you are not comfortable sharing. Just a little transparency can go a long way.

Using Your Relationships to Build More Relationships

I am not a big fan of social media, but I have always been impressed by how it is used to build both personal and professional relationships. LinkedIn, for example, uses relationships that you already have established to build more relationships. Social media companies have made millions of dollars simply through relationship building and the power of one simple connection. I have come to realize more generally that many of the relationships you build have the capacity to help you build more relationships that can also benefit you. Many of the relationships I have now were established from other relationships that I took the time to build and cultivate.

The relationships that I have built personally have had a tremendous effect on my professional life, leading me to many opportunities. My first job at IBM was the result of a personal relationship. I remember receiving a call from a close friend of my family who had an existing relationship with an executive from IBM. The company was hiring for its Big Blue program, and it was looking for young African Americans to join the team. The executive had no idea that I was pursuing a career in information technology, but my close friend knew that was my plan. Although this was just an introduction, it was the perfect opportunity to build a new relationship from a pre-existing one. After I was hired, I spent several years working directly for him at IBM and began to build a relationship that was stronger than the relationship that connected us originally. It is very important to understand that every relationship you build is a potential stepping-stone to another.

You never know which relationships will be the conduit to your next opportunity inside or outside your organization. The IBM relationship not only led to my first job but also would prove to be instrumental down the line as I began to take on jobs that required transformational change. Almost twenty years later, this relationship would pay dividends. When attempting to transform organizations, there will be times when resources are needed as tools to assist you through the process. I was at a point in the vision process where I needed to know how we would obtain funding because the organization lacked the resources for several of the initiatives in my plan. Without the funding, the transformation would undoubtly hit a serious roadblock. I needed funding for training and hardware that would support the transformational change.

Always remember that when you build relationships

you need to sustain them (which I will discuss later in this chapter). I was able to sustain this relationship for 20 years and had no idea if or when I would need it. One evening he flew into town for a meeting and asked if we could catch up at dinner before he left town. That night I was discussing work as usual and the vision and plans for organizational transformation that was needed in my current role. As I began to explain, I told him that my organization lacked the essential funding to implement the training and purchase the hardware necessary to execute the plan. He paused for a few seconds, smiled, and said, "I think I may be able to help you with that." I did not expect this response, but it was not a total surprise because I was aware of the strength of our relationship as well as its ability to potentially pay dividends. I always look to build business relationships that have value. I was able to use an outside relationship that was built years ago to help with the current transformation initiative I was taking on.

Develop External Relationships

Developing relationships inside your organization to aid you in the transformation process is important, but developing relationships outside of your organization is just as important, because outside influence can be critical to your success. Many times in my career, I have witnessed outside influencers have profound effects on decisions made inside of organizations. Working on any major project within your organization, I am sure you have heard this statement before or some version of it: "We need to make sure we include the external stakeholders before we move forward with this plan." Every single organization I have worked for has had this type of conversation when embarking on any major transformation.

There is a reason why external communications take place. External relationships can help move your agenda forward when they are chosen wisely. You need to be very careful when building this type of relationship because it can also backfire. I have been in organizations where one outside stakeholder influenced almost every decision we made as an organization. I am sure you are thinking that this is bad and wondering how anything like this could happen. Unfortunately this happens a lot in organizations. At some point over the years, the organization allowed this to happen. Sadly the road to changing this behavior can be long and tough. The biggest mistake you can make is to try to take this on immediately. Your focus should be on how you can build a relationship with an individual or group of individuals to help move your transformation agenda ahead. Sometimes your best strategy is to build relationships outside the organization that internal employees can see. Always remember that internal employees are constantly watching how you move, and they are forming opinions about you and making decisions about what type of relationships they will want to have with you.

When developing external relationships, avoid stereotypes and gossip that you hear (and, trust me, you will hear it). Internal employees who feel they already know the external individuals will try to influence you and convince you of every reason why you should stay away from the external stakeholder. Do not allow this to happen. I have faced this several times across many different organizations, and every time the internal employees were completely wrong or biased in their assessment of the external stakeholder. I call this inaccurate gossip. **It is very important that you make your own assessment and remember that you are not building this relationship for personal reasons, but that it is part of your strategy for removing roadblocks and accomplishing organizational transformational change.**

Over the years I have heard many excuses as to why I should avoid certain external stakeholders. Some of those excuses have been: The external stakeholders are difficult, unfriendly, unprofessional, mean and unreasonable. As a leader, you must examine the potential risks and rewards of what building external relationships could do for you and your road to transformation. Just as they are able to influence the organization, they can influence and remove road blocks for you once you have won them over. What most leaders in these types of situations overlook is that somehow the external stakeholders have elevated themselves to a position of influence and strength. Transformational leaders should confront it strategically instead of running from it. We need to learn how to use that strength to our advantage until we can completely eliminate the impact of the influence.

When entering an organization, always look to see who is influencing the organization from the outside. You cannot ignore this if you want to be successful as a leader. I can tell you from experience that every organization has an external influencer. As a transformation agent, it is your job to identify that person and find a way to transform him or her into a tool to unblock and advocate for the transformation you intend to make.

Strategically Build Lasting Relationships

Do not stop at just building relationships. You must build lasting relationships. Building strong and lasting business relationships takes consistent communication and interaction to keep the relationship alive. Continuously initiating contact with individuals is not always easy. Working in general can be hectic and does not leave much time for much of anything else. The last thing most of us are thinking about is going the extra mile to help sustain or build a relationship.

Keeping my 20-year business relationship alive and strong took a lot of interaction over the years. Look at how we build relationships with pets or other animals. We build strong, trusting relationships with them without even speaking the same language. How are such strong relationships built without true verbal communication?

All communication does not have to be verbal. Although verbal communication can be critical, I have sustained my relationships by using a combination of verbal communication, gestures, written communication, and listening. Over the course of the 20-year relationship, we did not speak as often as one may think, but we stayed engaged at critical times. I took the time early on in the relationship to find out what was important to him and what he cared about. When you are building relationships, it is very important to find out what is significant to those people and to use that as a part of the strategy to keep the relationships strong.

As you work to build strong, lasting relationships, it is not necessary for you to call or talk to individuals daily, but you must make sure that the interaction remains consistent. I would not let holidays, birthdays, or even information I had about sports interests pass without reaching out in some way. In this age of social media, it is very easy to keep track of these events. However, while social media has made it very easy to stay connected, it does not help you build strong, sustainable relationships. Long-term relationships can be tricky. Like me, you may find yourself in situations where you want the business relationship to last, but sometimes the other party may lose interest. Try to remember that may not be a reflection of you as a person but could simply be a result of not having aligned interests. Although I encourage you to build relationships in this chapter, I also want to make sure you understand that not all business relationships are meant to last.

There must be authenticity in lasting business relationships. Business relationships should be genuine. Both parties need to give and share information that takes them out of their comfort zones. As I mentioned earlier, when you are a leader and show humility and even some areas of vulnerability, it helps to build and sustain relationships. It is a risk that you must take as a leader. There are different levels of risk, and you should have some internal gauge on when and how much of a risk to take in different circumstances. You can be strategic and still offer some level of authenticity to the relationship that you are building.

When building business relationships, make sure that over time you start to look for shared values and goals that you both can identify with. We are often drawn to others who share similar interests, goals, and values. As the relationship blossoms, start to really hone in on what those similar interests are. You can do this by listening but also by strategically asking the right questions. Be careful not to appear as if you are prying into their business. Asking the right questions will allow for a more specific target to focus in on.

Because you are interested in creating long-lasting relationships that you can always depend on, it is important to develop mutual respect during that time. It may take some time for that to happen, but the entire point of this section is to focus on sustaining relationships. People need to see that you are impactful on some level. The relationship needs to continuously grow, and in order for that to occur, you need to continue to grow personally.

Importantly, you must be loyal in order to build a successful and long-lasting relationship. When the opportunity arises, show them how loyal you are and can be. People love loyalty and hold it in high regard when determining the level of trust they have for you. I have seen relationships defined by how loyal the other party thinks you are. Loyalty and trust go hand in hand. If employees feel you are loyal to them, they will trust you more. It is very important for loyalty to be seen. When you have the opportunity to show it, make sure you seize the moment.

As we wrap this chapter up, remember that building strong relationships is a key component in helping guide you through organizational transformational change. It is almost impossible to transform an organization without developing the right relationships.

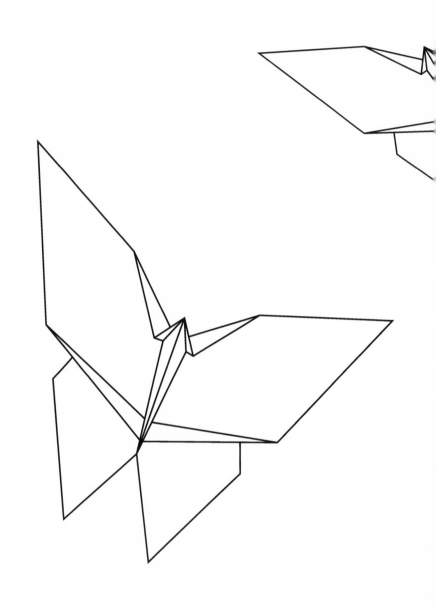

CHAPTER 3

POLITICS

_____

Be an organizational politician. A good organizational politician possesses integrity, honesty, compassion, and confidence.

I remember the first time I experienced politics in an organization. It was very confusing to me. I could not understand why I was dealing with politics in this setting. I believed that politics should remain on television news networks. I can remember saying to myself, "I really don't have time for this or the energy to combat it." I really did not view it as politics per se, but more like business drama that I could live without.

I frequently wondered why I should have to deal with such a headache. My initial strategy was to ignore it. I ignored it for years, and my production illustrated my failure to acknowledge its existence. Ignoring politics was not my best idea. Most young employees have no idea how critical embracing the game of politics is to the advancement of their careers.

At a certain point in my career, I walked into an organization as a leader, still not fully understanding how vital succeeding in politics was to my survival. Needless to say, I learned quickly about its importance. I walked into a struggling, billion dollar organization. This organization was struggling not only financially but also with its image and credibility. The organization was an operational nightmare when I arrived. Both locally and nationally, the organization had a dark cloud over it.

Employees of the organization lacked motivation and were very angry. They were upset about the mismanagement of funds and the lack of proper management oversight. Hundreds of employees lost their jobs because of years of mismanagement. To complicate matters even further, the new management team I entered into the organization with had no idea about the extent of the organization's issues.

Let me explain. On paper everything appeared to be fine with the organization when I first arrived. Remember in previous chapters when I talked about not making promises before you enter an organization? Well this is a classic example of what happens when you overpromise. Before I accepted the job opportunity, I was attracted to the communication which shared stories of organizational health and prosperity within the organization. While I realized that the organization would have some issues, I was not adequately prepared for the situation that I was walking into.

Almost as soon as I stepped into this new position; I was faced with a disappointing reality. This organization would not survive without making some difficult and impactful decisions. To compound matters, I had to make some of these decisions without fully understanding the politics and culture of the organization. Since you have already read Chapter 1, you can guess that having to make these decisions under the circumstances would come back to bite us before we really even got started. Imagine telling hundreds of employees that they are losing their jobs. Our decisions would affect family members of board members and our stakeholders who possessed strong community influence. We were very aware of the risk associated with having to make these types of decisions before we could firmly plant ourselves inside the organization.

As we started to make decisions about employment and structure, each department approached it differently, which was a mistake. It was important for every department to be on the same page as we went about making critical decisions that affected the livelihoods of employees. I have always been blessed to have people in my life who are skilled in the art of dealing with people and solving problems. I remember leaning on one particular mentor for this situation. I explained to him the situation and the first thing out of his mouth was, "What are the politics around this situation?" I told him I had no idea because we just entered the organization. I will always remember what he told me next. He said, "Stand still. Make as few changes as possible, and use data to keep as many employees as possible."

When he first said that to me, I thought to myself that there is no possible way I am going to be able to do that. My peers were making radical changes in their respective departments, and when we attended status update meetings on our progress, I did not have much to report. I would only bring the limited amount of data I could find to support my position on why all the employees needed to stay. Conversely, my peers were all looking for reasons as to why their staff needed to be let go.

As time went on, I stayed the course and continued to look for and provide reasons for why my support staff needed to remain largely intact. When we finally made a decision to pull the plug, I was able to retain most of my employees in my division. My peers, on the other hand, made deep employee cuts. This caused a lot of resentment, anger, lack of trust, and a considerable number of lawsuits. As a result of these cuts, the internal and external politics ramped up to the highest level I had ever seen. The organization hit rock bottom. To be quite frank, it was absolutely horrible, and I could not believe what I had gotten myself into.

In order to recover from this, I knew we would have to wade through the politics. I had to change my natural demeanor very quickly. I began to focus on key players inside and outside of the company, and leveraging relationships to ensure I remained employed. Everyone hated company leadership. We were marked, and every action or step we took moving forward was met with extreme scrutiny. We were out of chances, and we seemingly failed with the one chance that we had.

I remember one night talking to myself about how to find solutions to our problem. I was not a quitter, and I was determined to figure out how to fix this situation. I knew the first thing I had to do was to politically align myself with those I would need to help me, but that would not be easy. I had no idea who those individuals were. I knew optics were extremely important, and I made sure I was committed to not hiring any new employees outside the organization to help me. I needed to build trust in order for me to find political allies that would push my agenda.

For an entire year I watched, I listened, and most importantly, I found the political allies I needed to buy myself time and get me out of this situation. These political allies were trusted employees and community members. They had what I lacked because of time and poor decision-making. They had the trust I did not have time to build. They had the political influence that I needed to use to survive.

Seven years later I am able to say I survived this situation, and maneuvering through politics had everything to do with it. I was a part of an organization that turned itself around. I embraced politics and also used politics to digitally transform this company into an award-winning organization. I will share with you a few key principles that helped me through those tumultuous times.

Many people only consider the presence of politics in government affairs. However, politics permeate every sector. In business organizations, politics is about the complexity of relations between people. Complexity is generally characterized as something with many parts that interact with each other in multiple ways. Organizations are complex, and that alone is enough for politics to permeate through them.

Whenever there is an opportunity to establish power over something, politics comes into play. Politics can be very disruptive to any change or transformation when it is not handled effectively. When politics is handled effectively, however, it can be a real driving force in accomplishing your organizational change.

To successfully navigate politics in organizations, you must understand why it exists. For years I have watched many people lack an understanding of politics. Most employees run as far away from it as possible, but as a leader you should embrace it and learn to navigate through it. Navigating politics in organizations takes a strong mental focus and a deep-rooted understanding of people and their motives. You may ask, Is it okay to be a transformational organizational politician? Absolutely.

To transform organizations, you need to always look for ways to increase and capitalize upon your power within the organization. This may sound crazy, arrogant, and even selfish, but it is necessary for transformational success. Think about traditional politicians, who are masterful in the art of influence. Successful politicians understand their audience, and they are effective at problem solving and crisis management. A good politician also understands the importance of honesty. Establishing with your employees that you are an honest person builds credibility and respect.

Be an Organizational Politician

As I mentioned earlier, it is perfectly normal to act as a politician within your organization. Organizational politicians should possess the same qualities and characteristics of a traditional politician. It is not a coincidence that many successful business men and women end up transitioning into government politics. Just look at the last several presidents of the United States, for example. If you dig a little into their career histories, you will find that they were very successful corporate business leaders. The reason successful business leaders make good governmental politicians is because they were organizational politicians first.

A good organizational politician possesses integrity, honesty, compassion, and confidence. All four are needed to gain power and influence both inside and outside the organization. If you have ever studied the art of leadership, then you know that honesty is one of the most important principles in leadership. Establishing

63

workplace honesty fosters a sense of trust among the employees and external stakeholders, which you need to help the transformation occur. Honesty and integrity go hand in hand. When you have integrity, you are honest. As an organizational politician, use every opportunity you have to demonstrate honesty. Some people may see you as blunt or impolite, but they will ultimately respect that you say what you mean and mean what you say.

As an organizational politician, you must also display compassion. Establishing that you, as a leader, can show compassion helps you connect with your employees on an emotional and personal level. Traditional government politicians always stage some sorts of scenario that depict them as a compassionate leader. People want to feel connected with their leaders. That connection will show that you are in touch with the real problems and needs of the organization. It will eliminate the frequent occurrence of a leader being completely disconnected and living in a bubble.

Do not fall into the common trap of feeling weak because you show compassion. Compassion is looked at as a humane quality that shows understanding. If the compassion you are showing is used correctly, it can help you chart out the best course of action for the individuals involved. A successful organizational politician leads from the head and the heart. You must have the ability to see where compassion is needed in order to provide the courage to step them through it.

It is also extremely important for organizational politicians to exude confidence to the people they are leading. No one wants to follow a leader who lacks confidence in themselves, their employees, or the transformational process in which they are engaging. When you display confidence, you inspire others, which results in them believing in you and your ability to succeed.

Politics can be viewed as a dirty game. Sometimes the decisions that organizational politicians must make appear sketchy and difficult to defend openly. Oftentimes we fail to realize that the decision made may have been the best course of action at that time. Nobody likes to hear about backroom deals in politics, and on its face, it sounds really shady, but when you are an organizational politician, you must form backdoor alliances to help you accomplish your transformational change.

Use handpicked employees to build coalitions behind the scenes that convince others to support your organizational transformational change. This strategy works and can be very effective in cutting through the weeds to carve out the path for transformation. Time is always of the essence during organizational transformation. You need to take your time to form some type of understanding but also show progress around the change you need to take place. You will not have the time to touch everyone to convince them of your vision, which is why you need to strategically pick those in the organization who can do that for you. They are pretty easy to find because they are usually the loudest in the room. Find the time to sway them, and half of your battle will be won.

Survey the Political Territory

Territory is defined as an area of land under the jurisdiction of a ruler or state. Take this definition and apply it to the organization you are in. Look at the organization as a territory of land that you must survey for intel on how to tread through the transformation. You need to look carefully and thoroughly at the organization you are transforming. This will help guide you during the journey. Taking the time to do a thorough examination of what lies ahead of you is a necessity.

As I stated in my introduction, many leaders lack the

patience to really study the organization. I used to always wonder why they would rush to make changes. Leaders have this internal clock that they feel is ticking the minute they enter the organization. This clock has grounded many leaders before they ever had the chance to take off. You will not be able to control the terrain if you have not surveyed it. Think about when you buy property to build a house. You almost always have to survey the site before you build anything on it. Every part of the land must be analyzed.

This analysis is so important that it is an occupation with the job title of site surveyor. A site surveyor inspects an area where work is proposed to gather information for designers. If you build a home in the wrong area or on the wrong piece of land, it can have disastrous consequences. You can look at political territory the same way. There are a lot of similarities in what takes place before you build any structure.

You must be an organizational site surveyor by

inspecting the organization and the divisions within the organization where you plan to take on transformation. When you inspect an organization, make sure your inspections are very precise. Depending on the size and the complex nature of the organization, the time it takes for this to occur can vary. Do not rush the process until you know the territory.

When you survey political territory, the process must be organized and formal. The evaluation that takes place must include activities, measurements, and tests to determine who can help you accomplish your transformation and how you will accomplish this monumental task. The "who," "what," "how," and "when" questions must be answered, and the answers to these questions will help you understand the very basics of what you are dealing with.

Answering "who" will determine what employees inside the organization are best suited to help you with your transformation. It also determines who you need to steer clear of. Some of your obstacles will be apparent and some will be hidden. Who are your competitors? Someone wanted the job that you are in, and he or she will be out to prove that you were the wrong choice. Who are the outside forces that can aid you? Every ally matters when you are transforming organizations.

Answering "what" will determine the strategy you will use based on the examination and inspection that took place during your survey of the political territory. It will also determine what changes are needed for the transformation to occur. What must occur right away, and what can you take your time working through? Remember, organizational change can seem irrational to employees. Most employees will try to reason why this is necessary, and some will even question the logic behind the change. This is why the "what" question is so important.

Answering "how" will determine how you plan to operate within the strategy you determined in the "what" stage. The strategy on how to attack your organizational transformation is considered your compass. How will you accomplish your transformation based off the strategy formed during your survey? This step is very detailed. It involves metrics you plan to use to determine success as well as marketing plans to promote, tout, and communicate every milestone accomplished. It includes the development of the plan and then goal setting, which allows for short-term wins. Short-term wins are needed in order to keep the transformation alive. Organizational transformational change takes time, and often you will find that the team you started with is not the team you end with. This type of change will take its toll on the organization and its employees. Setting short-term goals allows for a strategy that employs quick wins.

Answering "when" is all about timing. Timing is critical

to the plan, and if it is not taken into account, it can have grave consequences for your transformation. This step is very important because it allows you to take advantage of situations during the transformation that may be advantageous for the change. It is very important that you remain engaged through the organizational transformation. Consistently remaining engaged will allow you to know when to and when not to execute certain strategies. Knowing when to act is not about luck; it is more about successfully predicting where you will be and what you will need at that time.

Understand the Players and Motives

For years in the workplace, I would always hear the phrase, "It's all about who you know." In most cases that phrase rings true. There are always players inside and outside of organizations that have great influence on the company's culture and direction. Those players do not always have to be high-ranking officials in the organization. Understanding the players and the motives behind the players is key to organizational transformation. You have to clearly identify them because in most cases, they have already begun internally processing whether they will be an avid supporter or road blocker.

There are several types of players that you should look for inside and outside of organizations. They come in all types of forms with different motives. Look for the following players and associated motives:

- **The Controlling Player.** These individuals want to control the outcome. They want to be recognized as the one who controls how the transformation occurs. They want to influence how business decisions are made. They can be found easily because they want to be seen. Many times, their voice is the loudest in the room. The controlling player also wants to control the narrative of how the transformation plays out. Shaping narratives plays a pivotal role in business as well as organizational transformation.

- **The Hidden Player.** These individuals move secretly throughout the organization and are not easily identifiable. They want influence and control, but they have no interest in shouting to the heavens that they have it. They may work behind the scenes to support you, but in most cases, they initially are working to sabotage the project. They like the element of secrecy and surprise. These individuals attempt to stay close to you and befriend you. They want to appear to be on board with you. If you can turn this type of player into an asset for you by winning them over, it can be a very productive weapon for you.

- **The Player No Player.** These individuals are like a mirage. They want to be influential, and they will try to impress you in every way to show they have influence. These players are a distraction and will take you off the intense focus you need to transform the organization. Their information is usually not accurate because they are doing everything in their power to appear as something they are not.

These three types of players have been the most common throughout my career. If you can first identify the players and then strategize effectively on how to use them to benefit your transformation pursuits, it will allow for an easier road to success.

Politics in organizations can be very complex. Organizational politics can be very frustrating, but as mentioned earlier if embraced it can be advantageous for you. Remember to first become an organizational politician. Reinvent yourself. It may come naturally to some, but if it doesn't, take the time to work on it. Survey the political territory as much as possible before you start the transformation process. Take the time to understand what the landscape looks like and where you need to step and avoid stepping. Do not enter the territory completely blind.

Finally, and most importantly, take the time to understand the political players and the motives behind their actions. This is not something you can avoid that will just go away with time. The players are real, and their motives are real. Play the game, or the game will play you.

CHAPTER 4

SALESMANSHIP AND CHARISMA

Charismatic leadership requires consistent focus and strategy.

A few years ago, I sat in a meeting with all my peers discussing a pretty normal agenda for the organization. It seemed like the meeting was progressing normally, but the meeting took a sudden turn that somewhat surprised me. We began to have a conversation about effective presentations. At that time, I was experiencing a fair amount of success obtaining funding for my initiatives, while others were being met with resistance. My peers believed that my road to success was easier and smoother than theirs. Of course, I did not feel that way. My impression was that I just effectively prepared for my audience. I took the time to study their agendas, and I appealed to them. It was a game that I knew I needed to win every single time.

Selling my vision and ideas was personal to me, and I took pride in my ability to convince my audience to buy in to my strategy. My peers were not very happy about what they perceived as an unfair advantage for me. As the meeting went on, one division leader shouted out, "The only reason you have success is because of your charisma." To be honest I was offended and extremely taken aback by the comment. I saw this as a targeted attack on the ability and knowledge that I used to sell my vision. On top of that, he made the comment in front of the entire team. I asked myself why he would say that about me. I thought that he and I had a better relationship.

That evening I jumped on my laptop to research all I could about charisma. I also asked trusted mentors about their perception of the word as it applied to me. About a month later, I started to realize that while the division leader did not convey it as a compliment and meant to be critical of me, the characteristic itself is positive. This was further confirmed one day while I was listening to a Ted Talk. The speaker was discussing charisma and how important it was to possess that skill set when your intention is to sell. I instantly started to feel differently about my peer's statement. I said to myself that maybe it was more of a knock on the others than on me. I mean how could anyone possibly sell a multimillion-dollar vision or idea without great salesmanship and charisma?

The short answer is you can't. I was so quick to be defensive without really taking the time to analyze what he said. I expressed and communicated the excitement behind my vision. I sold my audience on a dream, but I also had credibility because of my history of executing. At this point I would be more offended if someone communicated to me that I lacked charisma. It took a perceived negative comment to introduce me to a word that has now become a part of my strategy for selling visions.

Why Salesmanship Is Important

For many years, I often wondered how salesmanship connected with organizational transformation. It is practically impossible to transform an organization without the ability to sell the reasons motivating the transformation. Salesmanship is the art of selling, the ability to effectively sell, or to present persuasively. Persuasion is critical, and as a leader in organizational transformation, you need to master the art of convincing players within the organization to get behind your vision and goals.

To get the organization to believe in your plan for transformation, you must consistently reinforce it over time. Additionally, the members in the organization must see themselves in the transformation. As you embark on organizational transformational change, you will have several employees in the organization who depart during the transformation, and new employees will take their places. This turnover could present problems for you if you are not consistently selling the transformation to the organization.

To exhibit good salesmanship, you must appear extremely knowledgeable during your presentations. In some cases, the way you sell to organizations may also require some showmanship. Do not confuse showmanship with being over the top. Instead see it as something that will capture the attention of the organizational audience and help you achieve your desired outcome.

I have learned over the years that using too many charts, pictures, and PowerPoints can become distracting and may not aid you in accomplishing your goal. When you embed showmanship in your salesmanship, you are taking advantage of a different level of engagement to keep the message alive. While showmanship may not always be necessary to transform organizations, it is a good skill to have in your arsenal.

It may take some time to understand the art of salesmanship. The blueprints can vary depending on the transformation and organization, which is why it is extremely important for you to identify your audience. Salesmanship was a difficult skill set for me to master because it is not a natural part of my personality. Developing salesmanship can be uncomfortable and maybe even nerve-racking for some.

As a salesman or saleswoman, you must be willing to accept the good results with the bad. You will not win everyone over. There will be times when you are rebuffed and when you experience outright rudeness. Understand that it is normal to receive resistance. Your goal should always be to win over the majority. As you sell your vision, there will always be a small percentage of individuals in the organization that will actively work against the transformation. It is imperative that you remain focused when these small obstacles arise.

When you are trying to convince employees to buy into your vision, you need to approach it from their perspectives. Using this strategy will help you relate more to the employees' struggles and anxieties that are related to or stem from the organization's transformation. Employing empathy will also allow you to get out in front of any concerns before they escalate to a level that is unmanageable.

Why Charisma Is Essential

As I mentioned earlier, I am a true believer that salesmanship and charisma are linked. You cannot be a successful salesman or saleswoman without possessing charisma. Charisma is defined as a compelling attractiveness or charm that can inspire devotion in others. To lead organizational transformational change, you must be able to inspire those you are leading. I stated earlier in my introduction to this chapter that I was offended by the notion that I was successful because of the charisma I displayed during my presentations. Obviously my stance has now changed.

Charismatic people have the ability to make people feel comfortable. When employees are comfortable, their anxiety and fear of the unknown are eased. Charisma also allows you to exhibit your presence in any room that you enter. Confidence, body language, and charisma all impact your presence.

Have you ever witnessed a person walk into a room and completely command it? That person typically has the ability to confidently and strategically address the room. When you are transforming an organization, you will need to command the room with charisma that translates into presence. A commanding presence also allows you to establish authority and causes employees to respect you. Trust me, employees will test you as a leader. They will assess just how much you will allow them to get away with.

Charismatic leadership requires consistent focus and strategy. Do not confuse charisma with charm. While all charismatic leaders possess charm, not all charming people are charismatic. Charisma impacts entire audiences, while charm may focus on an individual. Charisma must be a part of your leadership strategy. A charismatic leader communicates in a way that is clear and very concise. You cannot exhibit charisma if you are not knowledgeable about what you are communicating. A lack of knowledge and the inability to concisely and succinctly communicate at will shows weakness as a leader. You must always come prepared any time you are communicating about aspects of the transformation.

It is important that you do not display arrogance while you are leading. People can mistake a charismatic leader for a self-serving leader, so always be intentional. When you are intentional about displaying charisma, you will almost always deploy a strategy with it.

Displaying charisma does not mean that you are the only one talking. **You must be able to listen even more than you talk.** Remember, charisma is about the ability to inspire others. Your team will need to be attracted to you so that their desire to work for you increases. The attractiveness of leaders depends on their level of empathy. Empathy shows that as a leader of transformational change, you can relate to and understand what the organization is feeling and thinking. Emotions are a big part of change. Can you as a leader temper emotion by stepping inside the shoes of your employees?

Charismatic leaders are service oriented by nature. They prioritize the needs of their employees. Your employees will have many needs that will change over the organizational transformational life cycle. When you show charisma and put the needs of those you are leading before your own, it will show your loyalty. The team will see you as authentic, which will allow you to have an impact on those who surround you.

Contrary to what most people say, all people are not born with charisma. Charisma must be learned. If you want to come across as a charismatic leader, take the time to study those who have mastered the art. You will notice that they effectively use emotions and beliefs to amplify courage and give strength to the team.

When you are a change agent, using charisma will help you bring about the change, loyalty, and faithfulness necessary for a successful impact. When my peer said that I possessed charisma, it was probably one of the biggest compliments that I could have ever received.

Take the time to learn how to display charisma. It shouldn't take long. Chad Perry, a Professor of Science at the University of Central Oklahoma, says that there are only seven verbal and nonverbal traits to focus on. Use stories and anecdotes when conveying messages.

- Show moral conviction when sharing messages.

- Weave subject matter expertise into messages.

- Set high expectations when delivering messages.

- Vocalize confidence in your messages.

- Use lists and rhetorical questions in your messages.

- Use body language, facial expressions, and voice inflection.

Science suggests that if you take the time to master the above seven steps, you can become the charismatic leader needed to lead transformational organizational change.

As you work to improve your level of leadership, use charisma to draw the organization into the vision you have laid out for organizational transformational change. Align the vision you have with a purpose, and you will see your change start to resonate within the organization.

When to Demonstrate Salesmanship and Charisma

Although it is very important to possess salesmanship and charisma, you must be acutely aware of when to demonstrate those characteristics. I touched on this briefly earlier in the chapter, because it is extremely important that you have a basic understanding of placement. As much as salesmanship and charisma can be very valuable skill sets, they can also lead to many problems if you are not strategic in deploying them. As a leader, you are equipped with many skills. The successful leaders have impeccable timing on when to use those skills.

I never had the privilege of serving our country in the armed forces, but I am very aware that they are equipped with a diverse arsenal of weapons to use when necessary. The army selects targets and then carefully strategizes on when and how to attack those targets. They have an understanding of the situation they are faced with before they execute a plan. They are masterful at gathering intel that guides them on how and when to move. In most cases they know what to anticipate before it happens.

I look at the skills we possess as leaders in the same way. Leaders possess so many weapons in their arsenal, but successful leaders use them strategically and tactically. One of my favorite books of all time is *The 48 Laws of Power* by Robert Greene. This book specifically discusses mastering the art of timing. There are two specific statements on timing that really stuck with me:

1. You must always work with the times, anticipate twist and turns, and never miss the boat.

2. Without patience as your sword and shield, your timing will fail, and you will inevitably find yourself a loser.

Understanding timing and anticipation is a unique skill set that comes with experience and laser-like focus. You have to be dialed in at all times. If you are not consistently engaged, you will miss the moment to properly engage the weapons you have in your arsenal. Timing and anticipation also intersect with the ability to exhibit patience and tolerance. You must develop a high level of tolerance when you are transforming organizations. I have yet to come across many leaders who think clearly when they are angry. You must remain calm and composed when dealing with a difficult situation or person. Organizational transformation work is not easy work. **Whenever you are faced with a situation that requires you to practice patience, use that as an opportunity to master it.** Progress can either be fast or slow, depending on the circumstances you are dealing with around your pursuit for transformation. As a transformational leader, you must have the grit to work consistently and steadily toward the goal.

Possessing tolerance allows you to lead optimistically and sustains your salesmanship and charisma. Remember, change will bring about emotional discomfort among many team members. I know how tolerance can help you with the emotional roller-coaster ride that transformational change will take you on. Using tolerance will help you perfect your timing on when to display salesmanship and charisma. Many punches will be thrown, and there will be many ups and downs during this process. You must understand the goal and keep in mind that this is a natural part of the change life cycle.

Your timing will suffer if you allow your emotions to affect your decision-making. Sometimes in our weakness as leaders, we think that everything is about us. We cannot get caught up in the cycle of bitterness or revenge, and we must always remind ourselves to remain hopeful, positive, and tolerant of the heavy lifting required for transformation.

Patience and tolerance give us time to think and respond effectively. The more I develop as a leader, the more I strategically use patience and tolerance. Years ago, a wise leader told me not to respond right away when I receive email messages that make my blood boil. This may seem pretty easy to do, but it is not. He said, "Type the email up and save it. Go back the next day and read it, and see if you would have responded the same way." The problem is it would take me a while to calm down, so the next day for me was no good. I needed more time. As the years went on, I took my time, and the results were amazing. This really came down to the art of timing, or knowing when, and having the ability to control myself.

Knowing when to use your arsenal of weapons means you must practice self-control. I often hear employees talk about certain leaders inability to keep cool heads. Your team will respect you for your ability to remain calm when prodded and prompted. No one wants a leader who cannot control himself or herself in tough times. When you can display self-control, it builds respect among your team. They watch your every move, even when you do not think they are paying attention. While your team may lose control, you as a leader absolutely cannot. Losing self-control will destroy your ability to lead effectively.

In sum, it is very important that you equip yourself with salesmanship and charisma. They are both skills that you can learn. Make sure you are intentional about applying them. If salesmanship and charisma are not used correctly, they can backfire on you by causing you to appear arrogant, insensitive, and selfish. Use timing, patience, and tolerance to guide you on when to apply them. You must remain engaged at all times to have a sense of the right time.

Organizational transformational leadership requires extreme focus and the ability to anticipate. Resist the bait that will be put in front of you to take you off task, and make sure you act at the right moment.

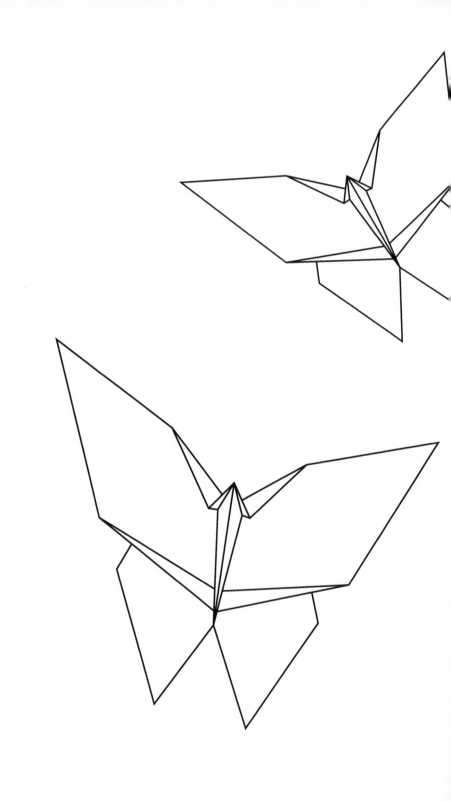

CHAPTER 5

BE INTENTIONAL WITH A NARROW FOCUS

To have an Intentional Focus, you must Understand the Organization you are Working for and what is Expected of you

As I mentioned in the introduction, throughout the years I have walked into several organizations that needed transformation to take place. Each one of these organizations had its own set of unique issues that plagued it for years. One consistent theme I found was that all of the organizations had several key decisions that needed to be made the moment I entered the organization. The issues that I faced were all considered important. I remember sitting in my office at times wondering how I would be able to transform this one particular organization with various critical needs right when I started.

Entering an organization when chaos is at an all-time high can be very challenging for any leader to take on. Add on the fact that important decisions must be made immediately, and it instantly can become overwhelming. How does a leader faced with all these decisions and challenges determine which one to take on first? Do you take on every decision that you are faced with immediately? Some leaders do. The organization still needs to run, and some leaders find that addressing all of the issues as soon as they walk into the door is a top priority.

My approach has always been a little different. Although you may face many matters that require decisions as you enter into an organization, I have found it very advantageous to always focus on what the CEO or your boss finds most important. All of the issues that you are facing may seem important to you upon entering an organization. This feeling is quite natural. Often in my career, I would hear the phrase, "You don't know what you don't know." This is especially true when it comes to entering a new environment with many unknowns.

Through experience, I stumbled upon how to navigate these types of situations. I am not going to sit here and give you some magical formula. When you are transforming organizations, you need a little bit of good luck along the way. It always helps when things somehow automatically align with the plan you had in mind without you having to take action to get it done. One day a CEO I worked for told me, "Hey, young fella, when you walk in here, you are going to be faced with a ton of issues and decisions that everyone is going to say needs to be taken care of immediately. They will make their problem appear as if it's the most important problem or decision on the table for the organization. Remember when you walk into organizations you have leaders over divisions and departments who are really only worried about their areas. Most often those leaders will not have a holistic view on what the organization deems to be most important."

The CEO continued telling me, "These are the specific areas I want you to focus on when you enter. It does not matter who comes to me and complains about you not handling their issues. I will always remind them of your focus." This was the first time I had heard this from any of my bosses. I was somewhat shocked and also relieved that she actually gave me organizational priorities. This type of strategy will also tell you a lot about the type of organization you are entering. This particular organization was a very strategic organization. It only took one instance of great leadership and valuable experience for me to understand that this approach is necessary whenever I enter any organization for the first time.

As we move deeper into this chapter, we will explore how to be intentional with a narrow focus. I used to hear the phrase "be intentional" a lot, and I really did not consider what that meant. You cannot take on every little issue that arises if you are going to be successful when embarking on organizational transformation.

What Does It Mean to Be Intentional?

Intentionality requires you to be purposeful in word and in action. It means that you make thoughtful choices and actively interact and engage. As I mentioned earlier, "be intentional" was something I heard at several leadership conferences and during executive meetings. Although I would hear this phrase over and over again, I could not find anyone who would take the time to define what it really meant.

When you move into a space where you are attempting to be intentional during organizational transformation, you must focus your mind-set on how deliberate you must become to achieve your goals. Your actions, vision, and direction must be clear. Don't confuse the word *deliberate* with *intentional,* as they can appear to have the same meaning. When you are deliberate, you are taking the time to carefully think about your plans in advance. When you are intentional, you are doing something knowingly. It means that you have some conscious design in mind.

To have an intentional focus, you must understand the organization you are working for and what is expected of you. Before you act, ask a lot of questions.

A transformational leader who is intentional always puts his or her focus on what matters the most. He or she will not be distracted by the small things or what may seem important at the time. It is very easy to get distracted by what I call organizational clutter. These are things that do not align with the organization's goals, mission, and priorities. When you have an intentional focus on what matters most, you ensure that it is reflected in the amount of time you spend on what is important.

When you find that you are unfocused, you must consistently remind yourself to get back on task. I try to write down my narrow focus somewhere that is visible to me daily. It's so simple but has been the most effective way for me to constantly remind myself of where my focus and priorities need to remain.

Believe and Find Your Champion

When I enter into organizations in need of transformation, I often find that those who are leading the charge lack the belief necessary to actually transform the organization. Leading is not only about believing in the people you lead but also about them believing in you as a leader. In most organizations, you will find many individuals who do not believe in what the organization is attempting to accomplish. They are employees who come to work every day to simply receive a paycheck. It is imperative that as you embark on transformation you employ people who are passionate and vested in what you are doing.

As a transformative leader, you must display and exude the confidence in the mission and goals that you and your team plan to accomplish. The art of persuasion is a critical skill set that you must master to become a successful leader. When you inherit a team that has a poor reputation both within and outside the organization, it really puts you at a disadvantage. The organization may not have the faith in your division, and this can make the road to transformation extremely difficult.

The lack of belief by many in the organization's different business sectors can also be demoralizing to the team you are leading. When most of the organization does not believe in the team or division you are leading, the entire team feels it, and it will negatively affect their morale. It is imperative for you to use your leadership to coach them up to ensure the success of your mission. One aspect of organizational transformation that I did not anticipate was the need to coach extremely talented individuals who needed their confidence restored after years of being a part of a team that wasn't trusted. **You will have to be intentional and narrow your focus to the areas of mistrust internally before it can transform externally.**

Most recently I inherited a team where the lack of confidence in each other and themselves was apparent the day I walked into the organization. They had been through a lot. The past year would go down in history as one of the most difficult years that any department in the organization had experienced. The minute I walked into the office, I could feel it without anyone saying a word. The division was even placed in the worst area of the facility. When you entered the area, it was dark and gloomy with no windows and poor lighting. Their position in the organization was apparent by where the organization physically placed them. I knew that restoring their confidence would be my biggest task.

Changing the belief within my team had to be intentional. I narrowed my focus on the hearts and minds of the team I was tasked to lead. I had to get them to believe in me, but that started with ensuring that they saw that I was confident and believed in myself. I started the turnaround with the confidence I displayed in the transformation we were about to take on.

Finally, as you move to change the hearts and minds of those you are leading, you must find a well-respected champion within the organization. What is a well-respected champion? This is someone who has shown himself or herself to be beloved, admired, and appreciated inside and outside the organization for the work and leadership this person has provided over the years. Every organization has an individual like this. This will be an important part in providing you an opportunity to make change. Simply put, the champion may help to give you a chance that many may not be willing to give you.

Never Stop Asking Questions

The older I get and the more I see in leadership, the more I am convinced that one of the hardest skill sets to master is asking the right questions. But this goes further. It is not just about asking the right questions but also making sure you ask enough questions. The one flaw that I had to overcome was making sure I did not feel intimidated by asking questions whenever I felt the need.

No matter how long you are in leadership, you always feel insecure asking a lot of questions. This can present as lack of comprehension, which can impact the perception of your intelligence. I had to learn over the years that this is simply not true. In fact, it is just the opposite. Asking a lot of questions shows that you are engaged, inquisitive, and set on making sure you have a complete understanding of what is being presented to you.

I used to ask myself quite often why we as humans are generally uncomfortable asking questions. I thought back to when I was a kid and all the times I naturally asked questions. As a kid, I wanted an explanation for everything. If you gave me direction or made even a general statement, you could bet your bank account that the next words out of my mouth were going to be, "Why?" or "How come?" Most kids are born that way. We come out of the womb questioning, but at some point, that changes and the questioning may be perceived as a challenge to authority or even as disrespectful. When kids ask the question, "Why?" the common response from some parents is, "Because I said so." It puts a roadblock up and stifles our innate nature that wants to ask questions.

When I was in high school, my mentor would always say, "Never be intimidated or manipulated." That statement has stuck with me throughout my entire career. I was taught at a very young age to never be intimidated, and I have always used that approach with my questioning. I never allowed fear to intimidate me or dissuade me from asking questions.

As you start to master the art of questioning, you must learn to be intentional about the questions you ask. When you ask the right questions, you are being intentional about the way in which you ask questions. When you are intentional about your questions, it means you have put in the time to study and learn as much as possible prior to the meeting or presentation. Have you ever heard the saying, "I only ask questions when I already know the answer?" When you hear that statement, it most likely means the individual has done his or her homework ahead of time. Leaders who ask the right questions and listen with intent manage and lead the best way.

CHAPTER 6

LEVERAGE WHAT IS ALREADY AVAILABLE TO YOU

When you look inside the organization for talent, you will almost always find a few gems.

When a leader walks into an organization for the first time, one of the very first questions he or she asks is, "What is the budget?" Most leaders are trained to follow the money trail because that will give you a good idea of what is going on inside the organization.

Once the budget is in hand, the next phase is typically an evaluation of the organization or division you are tasked to lead. This evaluation can take anywhere from three to six months on average, depending on how large the organization is.

The next step is when it gets tricky. Budget season is drawing near. You are a new leader, and you are eager to bring in top talent and make changes to tools and resources. I have not met many leaders who are willing to cut their budgets or resources. It is quite natural for a leader entering into a new organization, while embarking on transformation, to have many wants and needs. Those wants and needs can become really costly for an organization, and some of them will be denied. When I was growing up, I attended a school that had limited resources. We were well educated, but my school lacked the resources that other institutions were afforded. As a result we believed we were at a disadvantage compared to those other institutions.

Looking back on it years later, that simply was not true. I could not see it at the time, but the faculty and staff were skillful in leveraging what was available to them. I realize now that this was one of the first organizations I was a part of that was innovative in its approach to using the resources and assets that they already had available to them.

This chapter will focus on leveraging resources and assets that are already at your fingertips. Most organizations only use approximately 50 percent of the assets and tools they own. Year after year organizations spend millions of dollars on tools that require major resources without first looking internally to determine whether they already have similar tools. Leaders are so quick to look outside the organization for new tools and resources and sometimes do not really take a deep dive into evaluating what they own. Vendors are happy to sell new solutions and will take advantage of the organization's and leader's inability to understand their existing application portfolio.

What is an application portfolio? An application portfolio provides leaders with an inventory of the organization's software applications and metrics that illustrate the business benefits of each application. In order for you to leverage what is already available to you and the organization, you must understand your own application portfolio. During the next few sections in this chapter, we will explore different strategies to help guide you through the process of leveraging what you already own.

A Combination of Old and New

Organizational transformation is not for the emotionally weak. Your strategy has to be solid and should be customized to the type of organization you are working for - combining the old age concepts with new innovative ones. Having a mixed strategy when it comes to what you select and whom you select to travel this road with is important.

Your ability as a leader to attract and select talent is crucial to your success. There are some individuals who think that talent is not that important because of the leadership they provide. This is wrong. Take an example from sports. You have some teams that have outstanding coaches, but it takes more than that for a team to be successful. If two teams run the exact same plays, the team with the most talent almost always performs better. I am a die-hard Cleveland Browns fan. For years we selected many different coaches and players. This team had one of the worst records in the last ten years. Was it the coaching? The players? Ultimately, it came down to the coaches and the organization's inability to pick the right mix of talent.

Fast-forward to 2018. The team had one of the biggest turnarounds in history. How did this happen? The organization was able to bring in the right leadership with the right skill set to evaluate and select top talent. In one year, the Cleveland Browns went from 0–16 to almost contending for a playoff spot, largely because top talent was selected earlier that year.

I view organizations the same way. You have to be able to select the right talent. That does not mean walking into an organization as the terminator with the intent of "draining the swamp." Selecting talent that is currently within the organization is just as important as selecting new talent to bring into the organization. Institutional knowledge is a very powerful tool for transformative leaders entering into organizations. One of the first decisions I would always make when evaluating talent to join my team was to look at the talent I inherited within the organization.

When you look inside the organization for talent, you will almost always find a few gems. For one reason or another, they were either buried deep within the structure, or they were not used effectively under the previous leadership. This is a common occurrence. Sometimes the alignment is not there, and the fit is not right. This is not always a knock on the employee or the leadership. I have been a part of situations where the pieces to the puzzle were just wrong for that particular moment.

Bringing on new talent has its upside as well. Hiring new employees will likely help to energize the team. This energy will be necessary to help move a stagnant organization forward. New talent is advantageous because it also gives you a fresh set of eyes on the organization with an unbiased outlook. They do not have the internal connection to a person or initiative. For a short period of time, they bring objectivity to the table, and you must be ready to take advantage of it. Your internal veterans will keep you honest. They understand the landscape and can act as your guide as you navigate through the unknown. Both the old and new have value. It will be up to you as a leader to highlight those values.

As you look to transform organizations, it will be vital for you to understand how important it is to have a mix of existing employees to complement the new employees that you hand select. Always remember when engaging in this process that you are dealing with people. People can be unpredictable. This is important for you to remember because you need to be flexible and creative. From experience I can say that learning the art of managing people is a constant learning process.

Find the Waste

Every company has some waste that it is carrying. Waste as in, most companies lack mindfulness around their usage of certain tools and products. Organizational waste occurs in other areas as well—for example, not utilizing people to their maximum potential by squandering their knowledge, experience, and ideas. I find nothing worse than paying smart people, only for their talent to be underutilized. This happens a lot more than you would probably imagine.

How do we define waste? Waste is anything that does not add value to a product or service. How do we go about locating how and where waste exists? The simple answer to that would be to just observe. But let's go deeper. I want to caution you that it is almost impossible to completely eliminate waste, but you can do a great job disposing of quite a bit of it.

One of the first ways to find waste is to learn how the business operates. I talked about this in earlier chapters, but I want to reiterate that taking the time to learn and understand the business will help you locate where the waste is occurring. The waste could be in duplication and overspending, or it could be a result of the lack of efficient processes.

Learn the Business

How often, when walking into an organization, have you really taken the time to learn how the business operates before you started making critical decisions that affected the business? Your long-term success in any organization starts with your ability to learn the business inside and out. Learning the business never stops. The larger the organization, the greater the learning curve. The business can consist of multiple parts and pieces, and making decisions on small matters can often have a larger effect than anticipated. Organizations have several traditional business units: human resources, operations, finance, etc. Depending on the type of business, many organizations can also contain nontraditional business units that are given a unique role. These types of business units can pose a challenge and will require some commitment on your end to gain a deep understanding of not only the roles they play but also how they operate.

As a transformative leader, you gain a deep understanding of the business by asking the right questions. During my career, I encountered many leaders who simply lacked the ability to ask the right questions. I remember being called to meetings with C-suite executives who had no idea how to solve core issues or problems because their line of questioning was off base. I would often wonder how they were able to hold these high-level positions.

Learning the business also requires you to study organizational behavior. Organizational behavior is the study of the way people interact within groups. When you learn the behaviors of the business, you learn why employees behave the way they do in the organization. Learning the business and employees' behaviors can take time. This may not be time that you have if you are entering into an organization with an abundance of fires. A lot depends on the expectation placed on you as you enter the organization. Some of those expectations can, quite honestly, be unrealistic. Over the years I have had many unrealistic expectations placed on me as a transformative leader. At one point during my career,

I recall attending a budget meeting after being with the organization just over sixty days. Midway through the year, the division I was tasked to lead was almost ten million dollars over budget. During the meeting, I was asked to come back within a short time period to address the overage.

Let me remind you that this was not the budget I developed but one I had inherited. The request to bring the budget back into alignment was an unreasonable request at best. I actually thought the wrong questions were being asked in that meeting. Of course, I was wondering how the organization let the budget drift this far over the original budget. I wanted the questions to focus on the cause of this problem because I knew we would be right back in this situation next year if we did not address it. I remember trying to figure out how we allowed departments to spend eight million over the allotted funds. Where were the controls, and why weren't we having any conversations about that?

Do not be surprised when you are hit with unrealistic expectations as you try to follow this guide to organizational transformational change. The request will be unrealistic and very often unreasonable. Remember, as you are learning the business that you are also learning what is broken. When an organization is a failing or underperforming organization, you will find broken parts and pieces in every facet of the organization. You may not always be prepared to repair what's broken, but my hope is that by reading this section, you will be better prepared to address the issues that do arise.

CHAPTER 7

SHAPING AND CONTROLLING THE NARRATIVE

How often do you share the success that you and your team have accomplished?

For over 20 years, my professional life has been full of learning experiences. I can honestly say that during the course of those years, a day didn't pass without me learning valuable lessons about leading people. During my career, I have also learned about the importance of shaping and controlling the narrative you wish to convey. I have seen firsthand how leaders shape narratives in order to control not only the message they wish to communicate throughout the organization but also to manage the perception, both internally and externally, about the organization.

A few years ago, I was approached by a media company that talked to me about branding myself. As you can imagine, I was pretty close minded about this and wanted nothing to do with it. I had no interest in any promotional activities focused on myself or my work. This company was adamant about the value and benefits that branding and social media would have on my career. I could not imagine opening a social media account like Twitter or Facebook. Although I have been in technology my entire life, I saw very little value in using social media sites.

Some of my closest friends could not understand why it was such a struggle for me to create those types of accounts. This was especially perplexing to them because of my career path. One of my drawbacks was my awareness of the dangers social media sites could present to your brand. I never once took the time to look at how those sites could benefit my brand if used correctly.

As time went on, I eventually took the advice of the media company, focused on my brand, and created my first social media account. What I was not prepared for was the positive effect this decision would have on my career. During the first few weeks, my page was controlled by the media company. However, as time went on, I took complete ownership of it. I was able to see firsthand how using social media was positively affecting my brand.

It was not until about six months into this adventure that I really started to see how I could not only use this to positively affect my brand but also shape and control narratives. At that point I really started to see how powerful these tools were. One area I focused on was telling my story. Many times we go through life, and others tell our story and shape the narrative they see about us. Some people shape narratives about you without knowing anything about you.

It is very important that you take control of the story you want people to see about you and your career. If you do not, someone else will. In this age of social media, it is important that you have an online presence, but that is not the only area you need to think about. You also need to focus on how you shape and control narratives within your organization. How they view you and your department matters. Years ago, I would have never seen the value of having your own in-house communications team. Not only do I see the value now, but also it has become central for me in doing the critical and sensitive work of organizational transformation. When I enter new organizations and I am looking at the organizational charts, I almost immediately look to find the person heading communications in my division. If he or she is buried deep down in the organizational structure, that tells me how the previous leader perceived that department.

If you look at any CEO's team, you will find communications very close to that position. As you work inside of the various divisions you are leading, it is imperative that you adopt that same strategy for your division. In the few sections of this chapter, I will give you a complete guide and pointers on how to shape and control the narrative you wish to convey.

Tell Your Story

How often do you share the success that you and your team have accomplished? Most often in organizations, the loudest voice in the room is one of negativity. We all know that bad news travels a lot faster than positive news. Just turn on the TV to the local news station, or grab a newspaper and look at all the negative articles and headlines. Negativity sells, and for some reason, people are intrigued by it. With that in mind, it is very important to tell your story and to control and shape your own narrative.

This may not come easily for you. I found it very difficult to talk positively about myself or the work my team was doing. I saw it as bragging and did not want to appear self-centered. I have a few friends and relatives who have no problem talking about themselves or their work in a positive light. These people are extremely comfortable talking about themselves, their lives, and the experiences they have had over the years. Selling comes easy for them.

Telling your story requires you to know the audience you want to impact. As a transformative leader, you must think about who is going to read or listen to the story you are telling to shape the narrative. This can be an internal audience such as those within the organization or it can be an external audience, such as stakeholders. Most times you want to look for influencers inside and outside of your profession.

When you are telling your story, you must also work on keeping it concise and engaging. You must know what to say, and it must be organized in a way that makes sense and that your audience understands. I had someone say to me recently that I am a brand expert. I chuckled for a few minutes at the statement because I still don't see myself that way.

Controlling your narrative by telling your story is a skill you must continue to hone. Telling your story necessitates that you find ways to immerse your audience in the story you are communicating. When focusing on telling your story, you should always shape the message you need to convey around the customer's conflict or the areas of need for the business you are supporting. It is very important for you to recognize and understand where the wins exist for the business. Once you have an understanding of where the wins are, you must execute telling your story around the progress and accomplishments that you and your team are achieving.

Lastly, you must actively capture and document the positive wins for both you and your team. It's important that you organize them in a way that allows you to easily go back to them for reference. At times we can run with our heads down, going after those major wins, and often we forget to document them. Documenting your achievements is just as important as communicating them.

Socialize Wins through Change Champions

I am sure you are looking at the title of this section like what could this possibly mean? At one point in my career, I had a meeting with a very influential C-suite executive. During that meeting, we were discussing some of the positive strides my team had made recently. While we were walking through different agenda items, the C-suite executive told me that if I documented my successes, he would socialize them.

That was the first time that I heard the word socialize communicated to me in that manner. I paused for a few seconds and thanked him. It was not until later in the week that the significance of his statement really resonated with me. It hit me that I actually had someone with a great deal of influence ready to talk about what my team and I had achieved.

Finding influential people inside and outside the organization to communicate all of the achievements your team has made is vital to the success of your organizational transformation. Influencers, like the name suggests, have influence over others and are used throughout society, including social media, to promote and champion. Influencers are also valuable because in most cases they have an abundance of relationships and audiences that they can leverage.

Although influencers play an important role in helping you socialize your achievements, they are not enough to completely change the narrative. The message and belief in in the work you are doing transforming your organization needs to permeate from the top of the organization all the way down. We call this a top-down approach. How can you effectively communicate from the top to the bottom of the organization? You do this by strategically implementing change champions.

What is a change champion? **Change champions are individuals within an organization that volunteer or are selected to help facilitate change.** These individuals take extraordinary interest in the success of anything that has to do with change. I find change champions to be more important than influencers. Change champions are in the trenches, and they bring a different level of importance to the success of your organizational transformation. Change champions can be placed throughout all levels of the organization, and they work as evangelists for what you are trying to accomplish. These change champions are people who will speak publicly in support of the mission because they believe in what you are trying to accomplish with organizational transformation. Change champions can be hard to find, so you must look for certain characteristics in individuals to determine if they can be change champions for your organizational transformation.

What types of characteristics should you look for to identify change champions within your organization? Individuals who are open to new ways of doing things.

- Individuals who are very good at networking
- Individuals who tend to focus on solutions.
- Individuals who know the business.
- Individuals who are great communicators.
- Individuals who are not afraid to speak up.
- Individuals who are not scared to take risks

Once you find your change champions, you must manage them. As their leader, you must set expectations if you want to maximize the impacts they will have in championing your organizational transformation.

Change champions have roles to play, and just like a head coach, you must make sure they play their positions well.

Being Consistent Is Key

While you are leading organizations through transformations, you will not have much time to focus on controlling the narrative. We all know how difficult leading an organization can be without transformation involved, but it can be an uncontrollable beast when you combine leading people with transforming an organization. This is why it is important to find a specialist to lead the charge on all things communication-related in your transformation.

As I continue to progress throughout my career, I place more value on and see the importance of having an individual focused on controlling the narrative who is employed full time. If you want to control the narrative, you must have someone with you who can consistently focus on this full time. Consistency is the key to sustaining the narrative you are writing. You must have a high level of commitment to maintain the proper focus when changing narratives.

When you consistently focus on the task at hand, over time you will start to see the results you are looking for. Take the art of getting in shape, for example. When you start your workout routine, you will most likely not see major results the first day or even the first few weeks. You absolutely will not be in shape from just three weeks of working out. The results will come from your commitment to consistently work out.

If you consistently commit to the workout routines, you will start to see the changes you are looking for. **Transforming anything takes time, consistency, and commitment.** Transforming organizations and the narratives shaped around the organization's performance will not happen overnight.

Remember, consistency is the act of always behaving in the same way. You must constantly adhere to the same principles that are a part of the strategy that you originally designed. Simply put, you must stay the course. The big question is how do you stay consistent?

- Strategically design a plan.
- Stay focused on that plan.
- Make sure the plan is written down.
- Track and monitor the plan.
- Take one step at a time.
- Know your objective.

When you are consistently controlling the narrative, you develop routines, and those routines build momentum that will carry you through the next day. As a leader, your employees need consistency from you, and they will need it ten times over when you are leading through transformation.

The same goes with controlling the narrative. To

consistently control the narrative, you must fully dedicate yourself to the task and the end goal. This means you must stay engaged and eliminate distractions. **When you do these things and you do them well, you are on your way to organizational transformation.**

Made in the
USA
Columbia, SC